GETTING TO KNOW GOD'S WORD

How 66 Books of the Bible Tell God's Redemption Story

WORKBOOK

Dennis C Stevenson Jr

www.dennis-stevenson.com

ISBN 979-8-9875057-7-9

About this Workbook

How could a collection of ancient manuscripts tell a story that makes sense today? How could a writing process spread over fifteen hundred years and at least thirty-nine authors tell a story that connects? It defies logic that the Bible could be any more than a fragmented and disjointed mess of out-of-date exhortations and irrelevant stories.

In reality, the exact opposite is true.

This Workbook will guide you step-by-step through the entire Bible and allow you to understand what it contains. It's designed as the perfect compliment to <u>Getting To Know God's Word</u>.

As you read the book, this workbook will help you think through each of the major points and bring about a greater comprehension of God's Word. Using the workbook will magnify your learning and bring a deeper familiarity with the greatest book ever written.

It's my prayer that this book and workbook will spur you on to become a lifelong student of the Bible. For truly, there is no greater calling in life.

Dennis Stevenson

Let's Dig Into The Bible

Introduction

A (*Brief*) Overview of the Bible

Make an outline of the Bible based on the chapter.

1. _______________________

2. _______________________

3. _______________________

4. _______________________

5. _______________________

6. _______________________

7. _______________________

8. _______________________

9. _______________________

10. _______________________

11. _______________________

12. _______________________

God is the Author of the Bible

Genesis – Deuteronomy:______________________

____

Joshua - Esther, Acts: ______________________

____

Job - Song of Solomon: ______________________

____

Isaiah - Malachi, Revelation: ______________________

____

Matthew – John: ______________________

____

Romans - 3 John: ______________________

____

The Bible tells us that God, through the Holy Spirit, superintended the writing of all scripture. The Holy Spirit was the mastermind behind the organization and message of the Bible.

Introduction to the
Old Testament

Part 1

Introduction to the Old Testament

The Old Testament contains 39 books that span the time frame from the creation of the world to the return of the Jewish exiles from Babylon.

It is called the "Old" Testament because all of the books it contains are the oldest writings of the Bible.

Major Theme: _______________

____

____

Major Feature: _______________

____

____

Centers Around: _______________

____

____

Timing: _______________

____

In the Beginning

Genesis 1 - 3

The Protagonist

protagonist

[proh-**tag**-*uh*-nist]

noun

the leading character, hero, or heroine of a drama or other literary work.

How did Moses know what to write about creation? ___________________________

____

How does God's creation differ from our creation? ___________________________

____

____

What does it mean that God called His creation "Good"? ___________________________

____

____

The Point of View

Before God created the first human being, what two decisions did He make? (Genesis 1:26)

1. _______________________________________

2. _______________________________________

What rights did Adam have in the garden?

____

____

What restriction did Adam have in the Garden?

____

____

How did Adam discover he was alone?

____

____

As we read the story of the Bible, we will see it through Point of View characters' eyes. We will observe all of God's actions through the perspective of the people who were there to experience them.

The Antagonist

antagonist

[an-**tag**-*uh*-nist]

noun

1. a person who is opposed to, struggles against, or competes with another; opponent; adversary.

2. the adversary of the hero or protagonist of a drama or other literary work:

How is the serpent different from snakes today?

____

____

Compare Genesis 2:16-17 with 3:4-6. How did the serpent twist God's words? _____________

____

____

What influenced Eve to eat the forbidden fruit?

____

____

What influenced Adam to eat the forbidden fruit? _______________________________

____

____

The Conflict

In your own words, summarize the conflict.

____

____

At the end, where did Adam's allegiance lie?

____

____

What could Adam or Eve do to resolve the
conflict?_______________________________

____

Why didn't God just call a "do-over"?

____

____

Conflict [kon-flikt]

noun

1. a fight, battle, or struggle, especially a prolonged struggle; strife.

2. controversy; quarrel

The Promise

Consequences for Adam:

____

____

____

Consequences for Eve:

____

____

____

Consequences for the serpent:

____

____

The Promise:

What does "enmity" mean?

____

What is the "seed of the serpent"?

____

____

What is the "seed of the woman"?

____

____

How would the conflict be
resolved? _______________________

____

____

Gospel Application

The first few chapters of Genesis set the stage for the rest of the Bible. A great problem has been introduced. Now we need to see how God is going to fix this seemingly insurmountable obstacle called sin.

Genesis 2 introduces us to the Bad News:

____

____

Genesis 3 introduces us to the Good News:

____

____

The gospel is the ____________ of the Bible. It's the ____________ upon which everything hinges.

From here on out, we will relate everything to the good news promised in Genesis 3:15.

God Chooses His People

Genesis 4 - 50

Overview

The Bible refers to Adam as our "head" (Romans 5:12). That means that through his actions, he represented all of us.

How do you ratify his rebellious decision?

____

____

____

Given Adam's rebellion, could he fix the relationship with God? _______________________

____

Key Characters

1. Adam

2. Abel (and Cain)

3. Noah

4. Abram

5. Isaac

6. Jacob

7. Joseph

Cain & Abel

"Worker of the ground" = _____________________

"Keeper of Sheep" = _______________________

What is the requirement for forgiveness of sins (Hebrews 9:22)? _______________________
____

What was the basis of Abel's offering? _________
____

How did Cain respond to God's choice? _______
____

What do we learn about God's redemptive process from this story? _______________________
____
____

Hebrews 11:4

By faith Abel offered to God a more acceptable sacrifice than Cain, through which he was commended as righteous, God commending him by accepting his gifts. And through his faith, though he died, he still speaks.

Noah Found Favor

Noah's story shows us how God chose specific people to be the recipients of His favor. He worked through them to bring about the results that He wanted to accomplish.

As humans began to spread over the earth, what was the general spiritual tone of society?

____

____

How was Noah and his family different?

____

____

How long did it take to build the ark?__________

____

What was God's evaluation of humanity and what did He do about it? __________________

____

____

Abraham – Father of Nations

When God called, Abram responded. What did he display?

____

What were the 4 components of God's promise to Abram?

1. _________________________

____

2. _________________________

____

3. _________________________

____

4. _________________________

____

What did Abram have to do?

____

____

What was the effect of the strange ceremony that God performed?

____

____

Before this four-fold covenant, God had chosen individual people who lived righteously and walked by faith in Him. This covenant changed all of that. Now rather than God choosing those who lived properly, He had bound himself to one family line, regardless of how they chose to live.

Isaac & Jacob

Over three generations, God narrowed down and focused the scope of His attention on a single family. He bound Himself to them and promised them great numbers and a land to call their own. Through this one family, He would work to accomplish all His promises in Genesis three.

Could God revoke His agreement if Abraham's family turned away from Him? _______________

____

Over how many generations did God repeat His 4-fold covenant with Abraham's family?

____

What was the significance of repeating the promise to Isaac? _______________________

____

What was the significance of repeating the promise to Jacob? _______________________

____

The Proof is in the Pudding (Joseph)

How did Joseph's brothers feel about him?

____

What did they do to him? ____________________

____

Despite the intention of his brothers, what happened to Joseph? ____________________

____

In the end, what was Joseph able to do for his family (including his brothers)? ____________

____

Who ensured that this story had a happy ending – and why? ____________________________

____

____

God was holding up His end of the bargain. He had taken the children of Abraham, Isaac, and Jacob to be His people and set them up with the provisions they needed. Against all odds, they prospered when all others struggled.

Gospel Application

God showed His grace through the life of Noah, and then through Abraham, Isaac, and Jacob. He did not allow the situation to become hopeless.

What was the effect of sin on the human race?

____

____

What characteristic did the men in this chapter demonstrate? _______________________________

____

The story of Joseph hints at the plan God was working. What parts of Joseph's situation point to God's greater plan? _____________________

____

____

God Chooses Leaders

Exodus - Judges

Overview

Time and time again God's people managed to get into trouble. When they finally cried out to God, He responded by appointing a new leader to lead them out of their problems. But when the crisis was past the leader retired, or eventually died, the people returned to their willful way and another round of trouble would come again

At the beginning of Exodus, what problem confronts God's chosen people? _______________

____

What 3 actions did God need to accomplish to get back on track with His promise to Abraham, Isaac and Jacob?

1. ____

____

2. ____

____

3. ____

____

To accomplish this, God would call leaders who would move His plan forward.

Out of Captivity

Describe Moses' mixed upbringing. ____

What was Moses' major character flaw? ____

How long did he have to wait before God wanted to use him? _______________________

What great deeds was God counting on Moses to do? _______________________

What were the results of God's plan? ____

____

What was Moses' role in God's plan of deliverance? _______________________

____

God was on the move. He was leading His people out of Egypt. Moses, the flawed leader, had been used by a perfect God to put the plan in motion.

Into the Promised Land

Joshua was the model of a servant leader. He knew where his power came from. Joshua was humble enough to let God be big and strong. He didn't need to take power into his own hands and make the situation all about him.

What was Joshua's great challenge? __________
____

What was God's message to him? __________
____

Did God's plan for taking the land make sense to Joshua? __________________________

How did Joshua respond to God's plan? ______
____

What were the results? __________________
____
____

What was Joshua's final instruction to God's people? _____________________________
____

Victory over Their Enemies

What pattern do we see repeated throughout the book of Judges?

1. ___________________

____

2. ___________________

____

3. ___________________

____

4. ___________________

____

Deborah & Barak

Who was the enemy?

____

Who did God call?

____

____

How were they delivered? _________

____

____

What caveat applied?

____

____

Gideon

Who was the enemy?

____

Who did God call?

____

How were they delivered? _________

____

____

How was Gideon tempted?

____

____

The Consequence of Leadership

Was God required to work through human leaders? ________________

____

____

Was "the right human leader" ever a long-term solution for God's people? ________________________

____

____

What eventually happened to every leader God appointed? -____

____

____

How did the people respond when this happened? ________________

____

____

What did this reveal about the people? ____________________

____

____

Did God become weary of raising up leaders? ________________

____

Gospel Application

What attribute of God is revealed in this part of the Bible? ________________________________

____

How was God fulfilling His promise to Abraham Isaac and Jacob? ________________________________

____

How did God communicate His expectations to His people? ________________________________

____

What major question is raised by this section of the Bible? ________________________________

____

____

God's plan couldn't stop at miraculous deliveries and temporary leaders. We needed something that would work better than that.

Give Us A King!

1 Samuel - Esther

Introduction

These historical books describe the Kingdom period of the nation of Israel. This period lasted about 460 years and saw a new development in the civic life of Israel: transformation into a kingdom under the rule of a human king.

Who was the last Judge of Israel?

____

____

What did he do before he was called as a Judge? _____________

____

What was the scope of Samuel's influence over God's people? _____

____

____

Give Us a King!

When the people asked for a king what did this mean for Samuel? ______________________________

____

What was the deeper meaning God understood?

____

____

What did God tell Samuel to do? ______________

____

What did Samuel say would happen?

1. ______________________________

2. ______________________________

3. ______________________________

4. ______________________________

5. ______________________________

Then all the elders of Israel gathered together and came to Samuel at Ramah and said to him,

"Behold, you are old and your sons do not walk in your ways. Now appoint for us a king to judge us like all the nations."

1 Samuel 8:4-5

Saul – The First King of Israel

Saul served as a life-sized object lesson about how God views disobedience and rebellion. Just as He dispensed justice on Adam in the Garden of Eden, God also brought justice upon Saul, even though God had originally chosen him to be the king.

What do we know about Saul, son of Kish?

____

____

When his name was selected in the lottery, how did Saul respond? ____________________

____

How did Saul behave as the king? __________

____

What did Saul do to displease God? _________

____

How did God respond to this disobedience?

____

____

King David – A Man After God's Heart

Did David's father think David was a good candidate to be king? ______________________
____

What event pushed David to the national scene?
____

As God withdrew favor from King Saul and showed it to David, how did the king respond?
____
____

What kind of a King was David? ______________

What was David's secret desire? ______________

What covenant did God make with David?
____
____

This was the kind of king God desired. One who would obey Him and follow His commandments. God knew he would fail and sin when He promised to establish David's dynasty as an eternal line of kings. Yet God also knew David's heart and that David loved Him and would respond appropriately to His sin.

The Kingdom Divided and Conquered

Solomon the Wise King

What did Solomon ask for in the dream?

____

What did God give him? ______________

____

What characterized Solomon's reign?

____

____

Rehoboam the Foolish King

What did the people ask Rehoboam?

____

How did Rehoboam answer? __________

____

How did the people respond? __________

____

Two Kingdoms: Israel and Judah

How many kings ruled Israel? ________

How many followed God? ____________

How many kings ruled Judah? ______

How many followed God? ____________

How was the result different? ________

____

____

Lessons from the Kings

How do these history books describe the results of human kings? _______________________________

____

The books of Chronicles were written after the times of the Kings. What was its reminder?

____

____

What is the lesson we can draw from the Kings?

____

____

What hope doe Ezra and Nehemiah offer?

____

____

God was very clear to Samuel that He was the ultimate ruler of His people. However, He delegated that ruling authority into specific kings to administer in His stead. Just as with Adam, that delegated authority went awry, demonstrating that sinful human beings would not obediently follow God regardless of the circumstances of their lives.

Gospel Application

The futility of human leadership

Is it reasonable to look for hope or salvation in human governmental systems? _______________________

____

What was the downfall of the good kings? _______________________

____

____

Did the kings permanently solve the problem of Genesis 3? _______

____

____

The impact of human leadership

What happened when the king was godly? _______________________

____

____

What happened when the king was not godly? _______________________

____

From a gospel perspective, what need to the kings highlight? _____

____

____

The Wisdom in the Middle

Job – Song of Solomon

What is Wisdom?

Behold, the fear of the Lord, that is wisdom, and to turn away from evil is understanding.

Job 28:28

How do the Wisdom books differ from the History books that precede them? ____________

____

How do you define wisdom today? __________

____

What is the ancient Middle-Eastern definition of wisdom? ______________________________

____

What picture do the Wisdom books in the middle of our Bible paint for us? ____________

____

____

Job – A Perspective on Suffering

When the story starts, what kind of man is Job?
____

Why did Satan say he was like that? ____________
____

How did Job respond to Satan's attacks? ______
____

What was Job advised to do? ________________
____

What did Job maintain about himself? _________
____

What did God have to say? __________________
____

What was Job's sin? _______________________

In Job, we see the great lesson that our place is to submit to the great and awesome God. We cannot explain Him away. We cannot put Him in a box where we think we have Him figured out. Our task is to accept what He brings into our lives and be thankful in every circumstance.

Psalms – The Heart Relates to God through Music

The Psalms guide us toward wisdom as they direct our emotions toward God. They show that no topic or subject is beneath God's concern. Any trial we are experiencing can be poured out to God.

What kinds of emotions and circumstances are represented in the Psalms?

1. _______________________________________

2. _______________________________________

3. _______________________________________

4. _______________________________________

5. _______________________________________

What does it mean that a songbook is included in the middle of our Bible? _______________________

____

What do the Psalms teach us about the person who truly fears God? _______________________

____

____

Proverbs – Wisdom Nuggets

Who wrote the book of Proverbs? ______________

Why was he perfectly suited to write a book of wisdom? _________________________________

____

What is the purpose of the book of Proverbs?

____

____

What effect should reading Proverbs have on our life? ________________________________

____

____

What is bound to happen when we begin living under our own power? ___________________

____

The fear of the LORD is the beginning of wisdom, and the knowledge of the Holy One is insight.

Proverbs 9:10

Ecclesiastes – The Meaning of Life

The meaning of the book of Ecclesiastes revolves around the conclusion that Solomon shared in chapter 12:

"The end of the matter; all has been heard.

Fear God and keep his commandments, for this is the whole duty of man."

Ecclesiastes 12:13

Why was Solomon able to write the book of Ecclesiastes? _______________________________

____

What does the word "Vanity" mean? _________

____

Solomon explored every possible diversion or activity available. What was his universal conclusion at the end of every experience? ____

____

____

What is the only thing of substance that Solomon found?

____

____

____

Song of Solomon – Courtship and Love

When was the idea of human relationships introduced in the Bible? _______________

____

What is the common human expression in relationships? ______

____

____

What kind of picture does the Song of Solomon paint?

____

____

What values does it communicate? ______

____

____

On the heels of Solomon's conclusion that we must fear God because all else is insubstantial, we read the Song of Solomon. In this book, Solomon shares his wise thoughts on relationships and how to conduct them well.

Gospel Application

God must capture and hold our attention. Whether we are debating with skeptics or expressing our frustration at the proliferation of evil in the world, we must remain oriented toward God. He gets to decide what happens and what does not. His sense of justice is enough for us. We accept Him and trust in Him.

What counterfeit messages does our culture offer as an expression of "the good life"? ______

____

____

What is the biblical expression of the "good life?" _________________________________

____

How is God presented in the wisdom literature?

____

____

How does knowing Jesus influence our understanding of biblical wisdom? ____________

____

____

God's Spokesmen

Isaiah - Malachi

The Three Offices

Priest

What was the
purpose of the Priest?

____

____

Who could be a
priest? ____________

____

What duty did the
High Priest fulfill?

____

What was the role of
the priest? __________

____

King

What was the
purpose of the King?

____

____

How was a king
different from a
Judge? ____________

____

Where did the king
receive his authority?

____

____

Prophet

What was the role of
the Prophet?

____

____

Were all prophets
biblical writers?

____

____

Did all biblical
prophets predict the
future?

____

____

A Look at the Prophets

What defines the "Major Prophets"?

____

What defines the "Minor Prophets"?

____

What are the two styles of prophetic books in our Bible? ______________________________

____

When did the prophets live and write their books? __________________________________

____

____

What are the exilic or post-exilic prophets?

____

____

Throughout the books of prophecy, we see common themes being communicated. God's message was consistent, and He spoke the same general words whenever the people fell into patterns of disobedience.

Standards & Consequences

As God's people forgot about Him, they needed frequent reminders of who He was and what He expected. A common message of the prophets was to declare God to the people so they would know and change their behavior.

Note the prophetic messages in these passages

Nahum 1:2-8 _______________________________

____

Amos 2:2-6 _______________________________

____

Hosea 4:1-3 ______________________________

____

Joel 2:12-17 ______________________________

____

Zephaniah 2:1-3 ___________________________

____

How does the prophetic messages support Romans 3:23? _______________________

____

Faithfulness & Love

Note the prophetic messages in these passages

Hosea 3:1-5 ________________________________

____

Micah 4:1-8 ________________________________

____

Jeremiah 31:27-33 ___________________________

____

How does the prophetic messages support
Romans 3:23? _______________________________

____

How was God's faithfulness and love
communicated through the prophets? _________

____

____

Not all of the prophetic messages dealt with sin and punishment. Often God would remind the Children of Israel of His love and dedication to them.

The Plan for a Savior

Every year at Christmas, the Prophets come into focus. Their bold words promising a Messiah in Bethlehem remind us of God's plan of salvation.

Note the prophetic messages in these passages

Isaiah 9:6-7 _________________________________

____

Micah 5:2 _________________________________

____

Isaiah 53:1-12 _________________________________

____

Zechariah 14:1-9 _________________________________

____

How did God maintain a proper perspective through the writing of the prophets? _________

____

____

Gospel Application

How were the prophets received by those who heard them? ___________________________________

____

How did the prophets fail to provide redemption to their listeners? ________________

____

____

What heart issue did the Prophets reveal? ______

____

____

How is God's character revealed through the prophets? ______________________________________

____

____

And I will give you a new heart, and a new spirit I will put within you. And I will remove the heart of stone from your flesh and give you a heart of flesh. Ezekiel 36:26

Introduction to the New Testament

Part 2

Introduction to the New Testament

All the New Testament was written after Jesus rose again and ascended into Heaven. The earliest books may have been written as early as the 50's AD and the last books in the mid 90's AD.

How many books are in the New Testament?

____

What is the theme of the New Testament?

____

____

What is the major feature of the New Testament? _______________________

____

How do the New Testament and Old Testament define God's people? _______________

____

____

What is the New Testament concerned with?

____

The Life and Times
of Jesus the Christ

Matthew - John

Introduction

God didn't choose to speak through a prophet, priest, or king as He had in the past. This time He sent His Son.

How are the gospels similar to 1 Samuel and 2 Kings? How are they different? _______________

____

Chronologically, how do the gospels follow the Old Testament? _______________________

____

____

What impact can we assume from God's 400+ year silence since His last message? __________

____

____

How was this communication different from all the preceding messages? _________________

____

What is a Gospel?

What is the dictionary definition of gospel?

____

Why are these four books called "The Gospels"?

____

____

What bad news sets the table for the gospel?

____

What were the people of the Old Testament looking forward to? _______________________

____

In what way did Jesus embody all the divine offices? _________________________________

____

____

The Old Testament was looking forward to the coming of Jesus. Whether the writers or the people they wrote to knew it or not, Jesus was the one who would make everything right with God. Their faith was confidence that someday God would do something that would address the issue of sin and make permanent all the temporary cover-ups that they had been using.

Meet the Gospel Writers

Each of the 4 Gospels were written to a different group of people.

Matthew: _______________________

____

____

Mark: _________________________

____

____

Luke: _________________________

____

____

____

John: _________________________

____

____

____

Matthew, Mark and Luke are called "synoptic gospels" which means: _______________________

____

A Summary of the Four Gospels

Jesus Before Creation

____

____

____

The Miraculous Birth

____

____

____

John Announces Jesus

____

____

____

Satan Tempts Jesus

____

____

____

Jesus Public Ministry

____

____

____

Discussion with Nicodemus

____

____

____

A Summary of the Four Gospels

Rejected by Jewish Leaders

____

____

____

Jesus Teaches in Parables

____

____

____

Jesus Introduces the Church

____

____

____

The Triumphal Entry

____

____

____

The Betrayal and Trial

____

____

____

The Death and Burial

____

____

____

A Summary of the Four Gospels

Resurrection Day

____

____

____

Final Commands

____

____

____

Look back over the summary and identify:

The Pivot in the Middle

____

____

____

The Climax of the Gospels

____

____

____

Gospel Application

The gospels declare the good news of God. Rather than sending a priest, a prophet, or a king, God sent His Son.

The Gospel was God's plan from the beginning.

____

____

The Old Testament looked forward to the Gospel. ____________________________

____

Today we look back on the Gospel. ____________

____

What was the purpose in Jesus coming? ______

____

What did Jesus NOT come to do? ____________

____

The Birth of the Church

Acts Part One

The Two Promises

And Jesus came and said to them, "All authority in heaven and on earth has been given to me. Go therefore and make disciples of all nations, baptizing them in the name of the Father and of the Son and of the Holy Spirit, teaching them to observe all that I have commanded you. And behold, I am with you always, to the end of the age."

Matthew 28:19-20

Before He left and returned to heaven, Jesus made two promises that had not yet been fulfilled:

Matthew 16:19: _______________________________

____

____

John 14:16-17: _______________________________

____

____

The book of Acts shows the fulfillment of both of these promises.

Pentecost – The Church Begins with a BANG!

Before He ascended, Jesus sent the disciples back to Jerusalem to wait. What were they waiting for? _______________________________

____

____

Jesus promised that the disciples would receive power. How does the definition of that word change your understanding of the power of the Holy Spirit? _______________________

____

____

How would the disciples know when all this happened? ___________________________

____

The Jewish holiday of Shavuot was one of the three pilgrimage holidays for the Jewish people. Falling seven weeks after Passover, it was intended to celebrate the wheat harvest.

Once again, Jerusalem would have been filled to overflowing as Jewish pilgrims descended upon Jerusalem to celebrate and make their offerings of loaves of bread from the harvest.

Empowered by the Holy Spirit...

When the day of Pentecost arrived, they were all together in one place. And suddenly there came from heaven a sound like a mighty rushing wind, and it filled the entire house where they were sitting. And divided tongues as of fire appeared to them and rested on each one of them.

Acts 2:1-3

How did Luke discover what happened if he wasn't there? _______________________________

____

What metaphors did Luke use to describe what happened?

1. _______________________________________

2. _______________________________________

Taken together, what do these metaphors suggest? _________________________________

____

How did these events impact the disciples? ____

____

____

... Peter preached a great sermon...

Get a Bible and read Acts 2:14-40

Peter denied they were drunk. What did he show was happening? ______________________

____

Did Peter beat around the bush before getting down to business? ______________________

____

Was Peter kind or gentle as he pointed out their sin? _______________________________

____

What did Peter tell them they needed to do?

____

____

"And it shall come to pass afterward, that I will pour out my Spirit on all flesh; your sons and your daughters shall prophesy, your old men shall dream dreams, and your young men shall see visions."

Joel 2:28

... And the results were staggering!

So those who received his word were baptized, and there were added that day about three thousand souls.

And they devoted themselves to the apostles' teaching and the fellowship, to the breaking of bread and the prayers.

Acts 2:41-42

What was the effect of Peter's sermon?

____

____

How was the gospel spread further?

____

____

In one step both promises were fulfilled:

Matthew 16:19: _________________________

____

John 14:16-17: _________________________

____

Faith Spread to the Gentiles

As the church grew, what limits were applied?
____

Were these limits real or in the minds of the church? ____
____

What did Peter's dream mean? _______________
____

What did Peter's experience preaching to Cornelius reveal? _______________________________
____
____

Why was Cornelius such an unlikely convert?
____
____

Peter's Jewish companions, who had not seen the dream, were astonished that the gentile experience and result were the same as the Jewish experience at Pentecost.

They quickly concluded that the Holy Spirit had accepted the gentiles just as He had accepted them.

The Church Grows

Beginning in Jerusalem the church had spread throughout Judea and Samaria and was now entering the "uttermost parts of the Earth." Not only that, but the reach of the gospel was more than Jewish. Gentiles had, against all expectations, responded to the preaching and now were joining the church in ever-growing numbers.

Was Peter's story about Cornelius widely accepted when he returned to Jerusalem?

____

____

What was the official verdict? ______________

____

Where was the next "gospel outbreak"? ______

____

How did the apostles react when they heard?

____

____

How did the Church react to the unexpected spread of the gospel? ______________________

____

Gospel Application

How was the dynamite power of God displayed?

____

____

What was the role of the church? ______________

____

How did the gospel extend beyond just a "sin problem"? ______________________________________

____

____

How did the church embrace surprising diversity? ______________________________________

____

____

Such was the power of the gospel. It brought a new heart through the power of the Holy Spirit and it created a new people of God based, not family lineage, but on faith.

The Spread of the Church

Acts Part Two

Saul the Great Persecutor

Saul approved of Stephen's execution. His approval was the opening of great persecution against Christians in Jerusalem. The danger was so real that Christians fled the city and settled all over the eastern Mediterranean region.

Despite his zeal for Judaism, Saul was not from Jerusalem. What was his home town?

____

We first meet Saul in Acts 7. What notable act did he do? _____________________________________

____

If Stephen was the first Christian martyr, what does that make Saul? _______________________

____

Who was a greater danger to the early Christians? The pagans (Greeks & Romans) or the Jewish religious leaders? _______________

____

____

Saul's Conversion

Why was Saul traveling to Damascus? _________
____

How would you describe his encounter with
Jesus? ___________________________________
____

God had a plan for Saul What did He say that
was? _____________________________________
____

Who eventually accepted Saul and who wanted
to kill him? _______________________________
____

Who eventually taught Saul/Paul about the
faith? ____________________________________
____

Saul engaged in the business of his Savior with the same intensity and determination as he had previously persecuted Jesus. But when he showed up in synagogues to worship and teach, he was met with resistance.

The First Missionary Journey

Saul's ministry was shaped by four great missionary journeys across the Roman empire. As he journeyed, he changed his name from the Jewish Saul to the more Roman name Paul. This was in keeping with his mission to preach the story of Jesus to the gentile communities across the Eastern Roman Empire.

Who traveled with Paul? _______________________

What was Paul's methodology in every city?

____

____

Who was the first group to persecute Paul? ____

____

____

Why did John Mark leave the team? ___________

____

What did the Acts 15 Jerusalem Council decide about gentile believers? __________________________

____

The Second Missionary Journey

Why did Paul and Barnabas split up for the second Missionary Journey? _________________
____

Where did Paul's 2nd Journey begin? _________
____

Why did Paul divert his path and where did he go? _____________________________________
____
____

What problem did Paul encounter in Philippi?
____
____

Which of his rights were violated? ___________
____

Paul traveled through the cities of Greece and Macedonia. During this time, he planted churches and met with believers in every city he visited. Many of his letters, which we will consider in the Epistles, were written to the churches that he planted and nurtured through these missionary journeys.

Paul's Third Missionary Journey

The third missionary journey was cut short when Paul learned that some of the Jews in Greece were planning to assassinate him. Such was his reputation for preaching Christ and leading Jews out of the synagogue into the Christian churches, the Jewish leaders wanted to silence him.

What was Paul's purpose in the 3rd journey?

____

____

Where did Paul travel on his 3rd journey? ______

____

____

What problem did he encounter in Ephesus?

____

____

Why would Paul have needed to spend extra time with the church in Corinth? ____________

____

Paul at the Mercy of the Jewish Leaders

What was Paul's intention in returning to Jerusalem? _________________________________

____

What spoiled is efforts to plead his case to the Jewish leaders? _______________________

____

Who had to intervene and offer Paul protection from the mob that grabbed him? ___________

____

How long was Paul imprisoned by the Romans governor? ______________________________

Why did the Roman governor want to send Paul back to Jerusalem? _____________________

____

Paul knew that he would not survive back in Jerusalem. The leaders would find a way for him to have an "accident" that would claim his life. So he played the only card he had remaining: he appealed his case to Caesar. As a Roman citizen, this was his right, and it required him to be sent to Rome.

Paul's Fourth Missionary Journey to Rome

The Apostle Paul laid the framework for thousands of missionaries to come. His willingness to go where people needed to hear about Jesus has inspired men and women to leave the comfort of home and set off in danger and trials to deliver the eternity-changing gospel of Jesus.

Did Paul ever get to plead his case before Caesar? _______________________________

____

What did Paul do while awaiting his trial? _____

____

Did Paul let his captivity slow down his missionary efforts? ____________________

____

How does the book of Acts show the impact of the life and death of Jesus? _______________

____

____

"How beautiful are the feet of those who preach the good news!" Romans 10:15

Gospel Application

How did the Apostle Paul's life illustrate what mission and service looks like? ______________

____

____

Describe the global and multi-cultural reach of the church. _____________________________

____

____

Is opposition to the church real? How does it manifest today? __________________________

____

____

What is the role of the church in the spread of the gospel? ____________________________

____

The spread of the gospel also confirmed the centrality of the church the new Christian faith. Everywhere he went, the apostle planted churches. They served as the centers for worship, remembering Jesus, and support for one another. Through properly appointed leaders, the people would be led well and trained in the truth in which they had placed their faith.

Error & Instruction

Romans - Jude

The Uses of God's Word

All Scripture is breathed out by God and profitable

1. for **teaching**,

2. for **reproof**,

3. for **correction**,

4. and **training** in righteousness,

that the man (or woman) of God may be complete, equipped for every good work.

2 Timothy 3:15-16

What is the purpose and function of scripture?

Teaching: _________

____

____

Reproof: _________

____

____

Correction: _______

____

____

Training: _________

____

____

Why was such care and instruction required? _______

____

____

Has the church overcome such problems in the last 2,000 years? ______

____

____

The Epistles Teach Sound Doctrine

What do the epistles teach about humanity's standing before God? ______________________

____

____

What doctrine of Jesus do you find in Philippians? ______________________________

____

Did Paul's explanation in Philippians cover every possible question? Why? ____________

____

What do we learn about the gifts of the Holy Spirit? __________________________________

____

____

We find sound doctrine taught throughout the letters of the New Testament.

Doctrine means teaching that we affirm to be true.

This means that the epistles teach the truth.

The Epistles Tackle Error

Even though the early church had the Apostles, they still managed to find their way into all sorts of false teaching. Today we are no better off. We are just as likely to stray from the truth of God's word and need to be shown the error of our ways.

What dangers do we find listening to false teachers? _______________________________

____

____

What is reserved for those who turn from the truth? _______________________________

____

Why was Peter's hypocrisy bad? _____________

____

What topic did Paul address in 1 Corinthians chapter 5? _______________________________

____

____

The Epistles Offer Encouragement and Exhortation

What do we read in Hebrews chapter 11 and what impact should it have on us? _____________

____

____

What does John encourage in 1 John chapter 4?

____

____

What does Paul encourage us to do in Ephesians chapter 6? _____________________

____

Why do we not need to "defeat the devil"?

____

____

The Epistles are not all bad news and correction. They also encourage us that we have found something much better than we ever had before and that we are children of the King.

The Epistles Instruct in Church Practice

Since the church was a new institution and Jesus promised that He would build the church, He also made sure that those early congregations were instructed how to properly live as the church. The epistles are loaded with practical instructions for how the church ought to function.

What instructions are provided in the following books of the Bible:

Titus and 1 Timothy: _________________________

____

____

Corinthians: __________________________________

____

____

1 Peter: ______________________________________

____

____

The Epistles Are Not "Better"

How much of the Bible is God's Word for us today? _______________________________________

Why are the epistles easier to apply to our lives?

____

____

Can we find life-changing-truth in other parts of the Bible today? _______________________

Why might some people want to say the epistles are "better" than other parts of the Bible?

____

____

Is this an appropriate decision for a human to make about the Word of God? _______________

____

The entire Bible is word of God. It is not for us to pick and choose which words are "better". Only God is qualified to rank His words. It falls to us to accept all of the revelation and apply it to our lives.

Gospel Application

The Epistles explain the details and implications of the gospel so we can better understand how to follow Jesus. Even though the gospel had changed lives and given people new hearts, they were still prone to error and being led astray. The Epistles provided clarity and instruction to resist false teaching.

Why were the epistles necessary for our Bible?

____

____

What do we discover from the epistles in our Bible? _______________________________

____

____

What tension do the epistles encourage us to pursue? _____________________________

____

____

And Then Comes the End

Revelation

The Correct Book Name

The first verse of the first chapter declares what the book is about and its purpose. "The Revelation of Jesus Christ" is the theme of this book.

When was the book of Revelation written?

____

According to Revelation 1:1, who or what is the exclusive subject of the entire book? _________

____

How was it delivered and who wrote it? ______

____

____

How many different revelations are there in the book? _______________________________________

What John Saw

Describe John's vision of Jesus in Revelation 1:12-18

Clothing: _______________________________

Hair: __________________________________

Eyes: __________________________________

Voice: _________________________________

Face: __________________________________

Feet: __________________________________

Right Hand: _____________________________

Mouth: _________________________________

What does this image suggest to you? __________

____

When I saw him, I fell at his feet as though dead. But he laid his right hand on me, saying, "Fear not, I am the first and the last, and the living one. I died, and behold I am alive forevermore, and I have the keys of Death and Hades.

Revelation 1:17-18

The Things that Are

John was given specific messages to the seven churches. These were not all the churches in existence. We saw many other churches that Paul planted in the book of Acts. However, the number seven represents perfection or completion, so in these seven churches, all the churches of John's day (and through to our day) were represented.

Jesus' messages to 7 contemporary churches...

Why were seven churches selected? ___________

____

Were these real churches or mythical churches?

____

How would you respond if Jesus wrote a letter to your church? _______________________

____

How do the 7 churches of Revelation relate to churches today? _______________________

____

Messages to the Churches

Summarize the messages to the churches:

Ephesus: _______________________________

____

____

Smyrna: ________________________________

____

____

Pergamum: _____________________________

____

____

Thyatira: _______________________________

____

____

Sardis: _________________________________

____

____

Philadelphia: ___________________________

____

____

Laodicea: ______________________________

____

____

The Lesson of the Churches

Revelation chapters two and three stand as a testimony to us today for how we should function as churches. We are warned of the errors to avoid. We are told what our Savior desires of us. We would do well to take the admonition of these churches and apply them to our churches today as well.

What did Jesus value in the churches to whom He sent messages? _______________________

____

____

What did Jesus condemn in the churches to whom He sent messages? _______________

____

____

How could you apply this to your church today?

____

____

The Things That Will Be

Do we know when the Day of the Lord will occur? ____

How is Jesus revealed in the scene in Heaven?

____

Why is it significant that He was able to open the scroll ________________________________

____

How is God's judgment (finally) unleashed? ___

____

How does humanity respond to God's judgment? ________________________________

____

What happens after Jesus returns? __________

____

Following the messages to the churches, John was given a vision of certain things that were going to happen. These events were portrayed in symbolic and apocalyptic images that John translated into words for us today.

Gospel Application

Revelation ends on an optimistic, glorious note. God will dwell amongst His creation and those who have been forgiven will dwell with Him forever. And so shall we ever be with the Lord.

What do we learn about God's judgment? _____
____

How is God's glory displayed through the events of Revelation? __________________________

____

____

How do those who have received the gospel differ from those who have not in Revelation?

____

____

What is the impact of the blood of Christ? _____

____

____

Putting It All Together

Summary

What We Learn About God

Reading the Bible is an opportunity for us to see God in action. His actions reveal His character. We don't have to look at what He said, we can observe what He did. This is a much clearer picture of who He is and what He's about.

How is God's patience displayed throughout the Bible? ________________

____

____

What do you learn about God's holiness? _____

____

____

____

How do you see God's love manifest for us? _____

____

____

____

Great Takeaways from the Bible

How does the Bible present sin? ______________
____

Does the size of a sin matter? ______________
____

Does human effort offer any solution? ________
____

What role does faith play in our redemption?
____
____

Why is God's sovereignty important? _________
____

How was God's solution to the sin problems
simple? ___________________________________

____

The story of the Bible hangs together despite the unlikely number of human authors and the extremely long period it took to write. God superintended the entire book. That's the only explanation that makes any sense. Only if it was written from one mind could the story of the Bible hang together so well.

Take the Next Step

books2read.com/StudyTheBible

Learning about the Bible is a great first step. But what comes next? Take the step to learn how to study God's Word.

You'll find a proven study method that works for Bible students of all experience levels, explained in the same easy-to-read style. And as a bonus, you'll get a guided tour of your first Bible study.